SWIMMING UP WATERFALLS

A Playbook for Mavericks, Challengers
and Intrapreneurs.

Stu Lloyd

Wildfire Press (an imprint of Hotheads)

#swimmingupwaterfalls

7F Kong Ling Bldg. 100 Jervois Rd, Sheung Wan,
Hong Kong SAR

Cover design: Stu Lloyd
Cover image: Stefan Stefancik/ unsplash.com

To book Stu for a speaking gig or to facilitate a workshop, email stu@hotheads-innovation.com

We turbo-charge your creative thinking skills so you can innovate better, stay relevant, and find the future faster.
www.hotheads-innovation.com

Also by Stu Lloyd:

KILLER QUESTIONS – HOW TO SHAPE BETTER
QUESTIONS TO CREATE BREAKTHROUGH RESULTS

CONTENTS

A THOUGHT-STARTER
FROM STU.

It's a hard life being a Maverick. We're always swimming up waterfalls. Trying to take ourselves, our colleagues, our ideas, our businesses, to a higher place. A spawning ground where we expect to find more fertile ground and opportunities. Then we can bring these new possibilities downstream into our daily work.

This is not always guaranteed, of course, but we try our damn best to get there anyway. We stick our heads above the parapet. We colour outside the lines. We swing for the fences. We shoot out the lights.

But mainly we *do* stuff. The important stuff. The game-changing stuff. The life-saving stuff.

Because that's who we are. It's in our DNA.

It's the Maverick Mindset that sets us apart.

Otherwise we'd be like the rest – managers who are like spare tyres around the mid-riff of the bloated bureaucracy. Or passengers being swept along downstream by the urgent everyday stuff. And possibly going over the edge of the waterfall with all the others who don't see or heed the danger signs of digital disruption.

The metaphor of the waterfall is a useful one in business today. The strength of the rush of water is like the status quo at work. Hard to resist. Everything is urgent with your day-to-day line responsibilities, and you can easily get pulled along in the rip. And it's easy to just focus on that because that keeps you 'busy' which is the ultimate badge of honour for those who don't know any better. And we're all headed in the same direction downstream together so it feels alright, right?

But if you're not focusing on the right things, you and your company will soon hear the deafening roar of the water thunderously hitting the rocks below. The call to man the life boats. Abandon ship. Only 12 of the 500 companies in the Fortune 500 in 1995 – just 25 short years ago -- are still in the top 500.

So, you are a salmon. You swim upstream, against the tide, and often against the advice of your colleagues and your boss.

And, if you're still reading, this book is for you because you're from a different school (of thought, not fish).

It's a curation and compilation of the best (and worst) of The Maverick Manifesto, a blog which I take upon myself to write each week and share with my like-minded tribe. But it's much more than that.

I don't expect you to agree with everything that's here – hell, I don't even agree with everything I write! But I see it as my job to provoke and probe at the outer edges and fringes where the world is far more for interest-

ing and there's possibility for the creative, curious and crazy.

For it us – we, the Unreasonables – who are changing the world for the better. And the Reasonables get to enjoy the fruits of our 'crazy' thinking which turns out not to be so crazy after all. Just different from theirs.

Which is why there's always that resistance and push-back from them because they don't get it. Or us.

That's why we need to shoal together, and support and cheer each other on as we swim into the turbulent on-coming tide, while the others drift downstream bliss-fully unaware on their sunbeds.

Sometimes we wish we could be like them. But we can't be. Because that'd be brain dead and boring. Instead, we keep swimming to ensure the sustainable survival of the species.

Hopefully this book will reassure you, give you greater confidence, that it's OK to swim up those water-falls. Hopefully it'll provoke new starting points for thinking. Spark 'aha!' moments. Or get a conversation started around whatever's possible for you and your business.

I've included a handy Cheat Sheet at the back for you to reference and tackle the main provocations covered along the way, too.

So get your team and other sparring partners around, and throw the highlighted Playbook Questions at them. Some people make it a weekly Monday morning

or Friday afternoon thing. Mainly, have fun in your exploration of what's possible.

Good luck and swim hard.

Stu Lloyd
@RealStuLloyd
January 2020

THE MAVERICK MANIFESTO

(v1.0 2020)

1. We believe there are no rules. If there are, well, they are only there as suggestions, guidelines and starting points for thinking. We push, prod, probe, provoke, persist, prevail. Sometimes this makes us unpopular and difficult to manage, but we know that we will make a positive difference.

2. We believe Quantity = Quality. More ideas means better ideas. 90% of our ideas are shit. Only 1% of our ideas will be the earth-shattering breakthrough we're looking for. So we keep looking. And looking. In the most unlikely places.

3. We believe there is no creativity without down time. We sometimes throw our hands up and step away from the problem! Physical and psychological distance (and pina coladas around the pool bar) often help us see the answer clearer.

4. We believe most of the answers can be found in nature (literally and metaphorically). We

get away from our desk. We go for a walk. We smell the roses. We look to nature first because it has solved all the problems already.

5. We join the dots. We make connections to connect the unconnected.

6. We believe nothing is completely original. Not even this Manifesto. We've stood on other peoples' shoulders, tipped them upside down, and built on their ideas.

7. We believe the best solutions won't come from inside our domain. So we don't look over our competitors' shoulders – that's 1% marginal stuff. We look as far away from your domain as possible. Someone else has already solved our problem – we just need to find out who? So we meet people for coffees and lunches until we find 'em.

8. We sometimes get carried away with our own bullshit and our own Creative Genius. But others offer a valuable perspective, so we always ask them for input too.

9. We Break the Cage! We find the bars are usually made of glass, anyway. We colour outside the lines and sometimes run with scissors.

10. We Start Stuff. We do something to get the ball rolling. *Anything!* Creativity starts and finishes with an action step.

11. We Question Everything. (Including this manifesto. *Especially this manifesto.*) Because the status quo sucks compared to what could

be.

ON THE MAVERICK MINDSET.

What's *Your* Colour of the Year?

Pantone have just announced their 'colour of the year' for 2020.

It is Pantone 19-4052 Classic Blue.

But being a Maverick, you'll head for the opposite end of the spectrum.

Something like Pantone Orange 021C.

But being a Maverick, you'll ignore that too and use whatever damn colour you feel does the job best.

Because swimming against the tide is what you do.

It's tiring but it's worth it, because that's where you make the most difference.

5 books on Creative Leadership Mavericks MUST READ.

One thing I love most is browsing other people's bookshelves -- whether it's in their office or in their home. Because I think more than anything else it helps you to really feel where that person is coming from (and, importantly, where they are going).

The bookshelves in my office are overflowing with titles spanning psychology, military history, colonial history, behavioural science and economics, persuasion, communication skills, and creativity and innovation, plus a bit more creativity and innovation, and then a few more lying on the side about creativity and innovation.

I recently had a chat with a new contact in Hong Kong and he wanted to get a better feeling for where my head was at in terms of my take on creative thinking and innovation.

This forced me to think: what would be my top 5 books on the subject?

So I narrowed it down to these, which I share with you in the hope that you might understand me better but, more importantly, understand yourself and your creative leadership style, attitude, and skills, better:

1. Creativity Inc, by Ed Catmull (co-founder of Pixar). By far the best breakdown of what leading real creatives in a curious organisation looks like.

2. BOYD, by Robert Coram. Amazing story of a gutsy self-made man who challenged the common wisdom of combat flying (and the entire Pentagon thought process). Stood up to one of the biggest toughest bureaucracies in the world, and won. The ultimate intrapreneur. He invented the OODA Loop which is being taught in cutting-edge innovation programs to this day. How is this NOT a Netflix movie already? I love this guy and I might write the screenplay.

3. Mavericks at Work, by Taylor and LeBarre. A delightful collection of examples where fresh new thinking and colouring outside of the lines has created great big revenue opportunities or entire new businesses. Everyone is regarded as an outsider upstart ... until you're not. And that's the point -- the OTHERS just don't get it -- YET!

4. The Innovator's DNA, by Gregerson, Christenson, Dyer. Gregerson is one of my innovation heroes because he blends academia with practice-proven stuff that works in corporate reality (and Clay Christensen is no slouch either). In this book they study the greatest innovators and work out that there are 5 key behaviours that consistently differentiate them.

5. Originals by Adam Grant. He champions the fact that innovation comes from the least likely sources sometimes, but requires people to put up their hand even if it means going over their boss's head, challenges successful 200-year corporate mindsets, and is counter-intuitive (such as the entrepreneur who gives VCs reasons NOT to invest in his idea. Hint: it works!)

Of course, you'll be arguing with many of my choices, and wanting to draw up your own list. Don't worry -- I'm arguing with myself, too!

So, I sneaked in a #6.

Then it was whether it was **A More Beautiful Question by Warren Berger,**
or Freakonomics by Levitt and Dubner?

After arm-wrestling with myself, and playing "paper, scissors, rock" (best of 3 of course), I included Freakonomics, because they've turned it into a series of books, podcasts and a whole tribe of fans. And taught us not to take data at face value, and more importantly to challenge the data, and find the real soul in the story, with amazingly surprising conclusions. All wrapped up in great fun storytelling. Who woulda thought numbers could be so exciting?

So, that's MY five, er, six. What's on YOUR list?

My Top 5 Thinking Role Models.

Here are the top 5 people I admire for their different and inspiring creative thought processes:

Leonardo da Vinci (the ultimate trans-disciplinary thinker)

Elon Musk (Leonardo da Vinci of the 21st century, bringing his sci-fi fantasies to life.)

Nikolai Tesla (amazing brain, shit businessman)

Steve Jobs (for his zoomed out eco-system complexity thinking)

Guy Laliberte (Cirque du Soleil founder who inspirationally mashed imagination and business, and went from accordion busker to billionaire.)

I think what they all have in common is that they all have elements which cause us to dream and aspire beyond what's possible, and all re-imagined and re-invented the field/s they're in.

Your turn:

Who are the BIG 5 in your life?
How can you emulate their approach to help you break the glass cage of your current thinking, or see your industry from a different direction that could change the game?

The Freedom of Not Being a Sheep.

Growing up on a farm in Southern Africa was a wonderful childhood for me. The freedom to roam and play and explore as far as the eye could see.

Plus we had the chance to interact with nature and animals.

One of my favourite pets was a lamb abandoned by its mother, which we rescued and it came to live with our dogs around our house. It fully thought it was a dog. It used to run with them, chase strangers away with them, eat with them, sleep with them.

Until it grew big horns, and started throwing its weight around too much, so my father, George, painfully decided "Lambie" had to go back to his tribe on the farm.

One of my observations about sheep was this. Even though they had hundreds of acres of hills and paddocks to freely roam around on, they always walked the same way to and from their paddock every day.

And so the grass on that path would get slowly worn away, until it was a clearly defined path, and then it became a deep rut. And they would walk in that rut every day.

Our thinking and behaviour in the office often takes the same pattern without us realising it.

We do the same things -- whether it's marketing campaigns, budgeting, sales presentations -- over and over, even though there are many other ways it COULD be done. And soon we are in a rut. Convinced that it's the ONLY way to do it. Failing to explore the open pastures around us, which might hold much greener and longer grass.

I'd love you to take 3 minutes now, enjoy a cup of tea or coffee, and think about what ruts YOU might be stuck in? What behavioural patterns are you repeating for no particular reason other than it has become your habit?

Having been heartbroken by "Lambie" going back onto the farm, that story does have a happy ending...

Years later we were out in the field and wondered if he would remember us. So my father called out its name.

And sure enough, this sheep came bounding from the top of the hill, excitedly zig-zagging, leapfrogging others, and dashed right up to us for a joyous reunion and big hugs.

He didn't follow the beaten path that day. Because he'd learned not to be a sheep.

3 Surprising Things to Know about Creativity.

There are 3 things you should know about creativity.

1. Creativity is 80% learned and acquired. (That's right, it's not genetic, it's a behavioural muscle group you need to work out on a regular basis.)

2. Creativity is the most important leadership skill required at this time, according to the largest-ever global survey of CEOs (thanks, IBM).

3. Creativity helps you tackle today's 'problems' better while adapting and anticipating tomorrow's challenges and opportunities.

So how are you going to up-skill yourself (and/or your team) creatively in 2020 and beyond?

Hard work vs Heart work.

Hard work is a must, a given.

In all of the hundreds of biographies and autobiographies I've ever read, hard work was the one constant success factor whether you were a software engineer, a tennis player, a rock star, or an entrepreneur.
Without this, nothing will ever happen, I promise.

But ...

What if you add some special sauce to what you do everyday?

Try Heart Work as well.
Come from a place of deep personal human passion.
You'll find your output and your outcomes explode exponentially.
Don't just go through the motions.

Go through the *emotions* as well.

What do you stand for?

Creative confidence is an important part of not being afraid of putting up your hand, and showing up.

A recent participant in a creativity workshop I ran in Malaysia had two tattoos emblazoned on his forearms to remind him every day of the career decision he'd made to get into movie production.

Several years later, he's blazing along.

Because he burnt the boats. In his mind, there was no going back.

That's commitment.

What are YOU committed to?
What would YOUR tattoo/s say if you got one done?

<u>Where Passion Comes From.</u>

"Each time you pick up a guitar, play it like it's the last time," sublime guitar virtuoso and Rock God, Eric Clapton, advises us.

That's where passion comes from.

Each time you make love with your husband/wife/ partner. Same.

And the same applies with every presentation and proposal you make at work.

Enable your audience to *feel* your underlying belief in, and passion for, that thing.

Because selling (whether it's widgets or your latest budget proposal) is simply the transfer of enthusiasm.

So make it count. Move the needle.

Stop faking it. Feel it. Make your *audience* feel it.
Otherwise it might be the last time you get a chance to play to them. Then there'll be tears in heaven.

ON PURPOSE & CULTURE.

What Comes After IQ and EQ?

IQ was the metric we measured ourselves (or others measured us) by since 1904.

Then came EQ, first mentioned in a 1964 psychology paper but popularised by Daniel Goleman in 1995.

So what comes next?

Soul Quotient.

Say what???

Hear me out.

Soul Quotient is the measurement of how individuals and companies embody and express their values, their purpose, and their humanity.

'SQ' also reflects how individuals and companies are able to create and engage and align tribes and communities because of their compelling vision and resonance.

Brands **like LUSH or Toms or Tesla might** be said to have high SQ.

Entrepreneurs like Jessica Alba, Mike Cannon-Brookes, and Ray Dalio might be said to have high SQ.

All businesses that thrive in the future will look a lot more like the social entrepreneurships of today, with a meaningful purpose at their core.

Unilever are moving in this direction with "sustainable living brands". Their research shows that 2/3 of consumers around the world say they choose brands because of their stand on social issues; and over 90% of millennials say they would switch brands for one which champions a cause.

Millennials are already the biggest segment of employees in the USA and will constitute 35% of the global workforce by next year. Nine out of 10 millennials live in emerging markets so Asia will be very heavily impacted.

Their spending power will surpass that of Gen X next year too, and continue to rise and rise. This will make them the most powerful segment both as consumers and as employees.

This means that they will shape businesses from the outside and from the inside, based on the desirability of their product/service offering, and their desirability as workplaces.

In 2018, Unilever's 28 Sustainable Living Brands – 28 of them – grew 69% faster than the rest of their business. "We believe the evidence is clear and compelling that brands with purpose grow," said Alan Jope, CEO. "Purpose creates relevance for a brand, it drives talkability, builds penetration and reduces price elasticity. In fact, we believe this so strongly that we are prepared to commit that in the future, every Unilever brand will be a brand with purpose."

This resonates with the zeitgeist because millennials expect -- indeed, *demand* -- more 'meaningful' interchanges and exchanges for their labour. And will call out companies that they see breaching the 'woke code' (I just coined that expression because no other phrase seemed to describe that new state).

Authenticity, congruency and vulnerability will be to the fore,

individually and corporately, wrapped around that purposeful core.

So, hand me the microphone, Mr Goleman. Great job, but I'll take from here, thanks.

Policies vs Principles.

Policies vs Principles – two different management styles.
Policies *prevent* downside losses.
Principles *promote* upside gains.
The key is in the verb because that creates the mindset.
So, how are you running your team or business there?
Which style do you use and how that may be hurting your company's creative cultural development?

I believe JFK is the other hero of the Apollo 11 mission. Here's why ...

50 years ago, I was sitting on my father George's knee, looking up at the glowing moon. He steadied the huge and heavy Yashica binoculars for me, focussing on the cratered lunar surface, as I convinced myself I could actually see Neil Armstrong and Buzz Aldrin walking on the moon.

All the attention on this anniversary of Apollo 11 is on those three ultra-brave men who went to the moon and back. But I'd like to zoom out and applaud something that happened eight years earlier ...

Because for me, the other real hero of this story is President JFK, the architect of the vision who made the Apollo missions possible. (Those who know me, know it's not often I applaud politicians.)

His speech to congress on May 25 1961 galvanized a nation. Lit the fires of innovation. And sparked the imagination in a generation of kids.

The most rousing part was this:

"I believe that this nation should commit itself to achieving the goal, before this decade is out, of landing a man on the moon and returning him safely to the Earth. No single space project in this period will be more impressive to mankind, or more important for the long-range exploration of space; and none will be so difficult or expensive to accomplish."

As a piece of leadership rhetoric -- equally applicable to YOU as a creative leader -- it is sublime for several compelling reasons:

1. Use of the phrase "I believe" tells you his personal worldview, and makes it deeply personal.
2. He's set us all a collective goal. Not just for the NASA boffins and a few propeller-heads. This is ALL OF US together against those pesky competitive cosmonauts.
3. The humanisation of not just landing technology on the moon, but "a man" who may or may not make it safely back home to his family a few days later. Now he's thrown a vulnerability into this mission -- success is not a certainty. How must the astronaut feel? How must his wife and children feel? Now we're fully emotionally invested in this.
4. "Impressive to mankind" imparts huge universal prestige and importance to this mission for generations beyond.
5. "None will be so difficult or expensive to accomplish" justifies any amount of budget being thrown at this exercise because it's now become a matter of national pride and human safety, deflecting our attention away from the multiple millions being fun-

nelled into this program. Plus he's reinforced the challenge, the obstacle so essential to a page-turning "how is this going to end?" storyline.

6. Plus, importantly, a deadline invokes a sense of urgency to make this vision a reality. "Before this decade is out." So we all know how much time we've got. The clock is ticking. Get on with it.

I'd encourage you grab your tea or coffee now, view the video of the man in action delivering his speech, or read the full speech text, and understand its brilliance in the context of the times.

And see how you can align your team behind you on the important mission that you and they are currently on by creating and articulating a compelling vision that they are dying to be part of. Give it a fizzing sense of something that rises well above business as usual, otherwise that's how it will be treated.

See if you can make it a speech for the ages. Give us something that we might be talking about in 5, 10, or even 50 years from now.

Tip: start with "I believe ..." and go from there.

Liar, Liar, Pants on Fire.

I imagine I was no older than 10 or 11 years old, playing with my brothers and our neighbours -- the Leith Brothers -- after school, like we did most days.

But this day was different because we'd found a box of matches lying in the grass beside the road.

We then did what most curious schoolboys would do: see what happens when you set fire to the nearest thing.

Unfortunately, the nearest thing to us was a sugar-cane field. It was that time of year where the cane was fully grown (certainly way taller than us) and the leaves brown and dry.

I struck a match, and held it to the nearest leaf. It sparked and crackled and was soon aflame. Nice! We stomped out the little flame. Now everyone wanted a turn. Matches were lit, leaves caught fire. We stomped it out. Great fun!

And then came my turn again. I held the match to a bunch of leaves, and suddenly the next leaves caught fire, and the ones next to those. We slapped, and stamped, and swiped at the leaves. But all it did was send sparks into the neighbouring stalks.

Sh*t!

Some of the boys pulled off their shirts and swatted the flames with them, but this just fanned them further. The hissing, crackling and popping of the flames in the cane grew bigger and louder. It was a real runaway fire.

Brainwave: you guys go run for some water. The nearest tap was down near our house over 100 metres away. No hose would reach that far. So we all ferried cups and dishes and buckets from the tap to the fire, which was by now running angrily across the field.

I remember the nervous panic. I knew we were losing this battle.

By the time a farm truck arrived, full of workers with hessian sacks to beat the flames, and some hoses and pumps that sucked water out of our swimming pool, I felt the end of the world (at least my world) was near.

We were no strangers to trouble, but this was unimaginably *BIG* trouble. Because by now nearly a whole football field's worth of valuable sugar cane had been burned, with thousands more acres at risk.

And the troubles only got bigger when a looming figure stepped out of a pick-up truck which pulled to a halt next to us.

It was Mr Potgieter. Sh*t! *Double sh*t!*
What you need to understand is that Mr Potgieter was a big, muscular man with a big bushy moustache, a World War 2 veteran no less, with a stern manner at the best of times, and even sterner when schoolboys were burning down his farm. In his hand was a rattan cane.

As the farm workers battled the fire, he rounded us all up, sizing us up with his beady eyes, looking us over one by one. That was nearly enough to make me pee my little pants.

"Ok, who started this fire?" he barked, waving his cane around menacingly.

There was silence. We all studied our toes and the ground with sudden amazing interest.

After what seemed like several minutes, but what was probably only several seconds of awkward silence, a little high-pitched voice stuttered from the back of the pack.
"M, m, m, me, sir."
It was *my* voice.
More silence.
"Step forward, Lloyd."

This can only mean the beating from hell, I thought, as I stepped through my brothers towards him.

Then suddenly his angry face turned to a big beaming grin.

"See that? This boy is honest. He has owned up."

By now my eyes were watery. Not from the smoke as much as being overcome with emotion.

"Well done, that's a good thing you've done in owning up there," Mr Potgieter said, patting me on the shoulder. Phew! I couldn't believe I wasn't going to be receiving a thrashing. Instead, I was being praised for my bravery and honesty.

Of course, Mr Potgieter reported this incident to my parents when they got home. And the whole farming community soon heard of the fire. But the story Mr Potgieter was telling was not of the sugar cane lost, but of this honest young boy who dared to face him, step forward and accept responsibility.

The memory of that day remains firmly etched in my mind. Not just the dangerous events, but more the lesson learned.

I learned that it pays to be honest. That was a major life-long lesson.

It has shaped and informed my personal and professional decision making ever since. Because every time

I'm in a situation thinking 'Do I tell the truth and own this, or try to fabricate an excuse?' or 'Can I mark up this invoice to client more?' I instinctively default to taking the honesty route.

Sometimes it's more expensive (and painful) in the shorter term, but it's always more rewarding in the longer term. Because honesty pays. You have your integrity intact. And that's priceless.

So how does this relate to you, your personal brand, and your professional dealings?

What stories do YOU have to define who you are, who you've become, what you stand for, how you live, and how you make decisions?

Having a story bank of such examples helps define you, and gives you ready-made illustrations to use. Otherwise, you're stuck with pleading that 'honesty' is an important value to you. You're telling it, not showing it.

Show your values with real and relevant stories.

Over to you ...

You Won't Believe Some of These Job Titles.

When I first started doing innovation consultancy work, having come out of 18 years of international ad agency life, my first feeling was one of relief and freedom. Not just because of the money in my pocket from the sale of my agency to a Wall St listed company, but because -- with my own one-man-show -- I was working with a blank slate again.

Which meant I wasn't weighed down by legacy thinking and the old "how I SHOULD do things" that corporate life often dictates to you. For example, I once got a stern knitted-eyebrow look from the network's Regional President when I posted a sign on my office door which read: **CHIEF FIREFIGHTER.** "Well, that's what I really do around here," I protested. "That's where I add value, because no one needs me when things are running smoothly."

In my own business I became the coffee boy, the assistant typist, the marketing intern, etc. I'm all those things, and occasionally I help senior clients to disrupt their own thinking and rethink their businesses.

Around that time I read a quote from Picasso: *"Every act of creation is at first an act of destruction."*

Aha! That was it. And I bestowed upon myself the grand title, **DAMAGING DIRECTOR**.

That then evolved into **Chief Hothead**, when that business became Hotheads Innovation. And I then added **Top Dog** when I started our storytelling brand, CATMATDOG.

And I always enjoy the reaction those titles get when I'm introduced at a conference keynote or panel. (Trust me, I've been called worse!)

Mainly I think the value in a job title is to tell the world a little about what you *actually* do, but also to evoke a feeling that YOU are the right person to be doing that thing for them. But more importantly, it frames the expectations of your own day's work. It says something about your *WHY*.

Aaron Levie, the founder of Box, goes by the title **LEAD MAGICIAN**. That conjures a great image of how he sees himself and his company's file-sharing solutions, doesn't it?

John Seely Brown, legendary former director of the PARC Research Center, board director of Amazon, etc, positions himself in his own company as **CHIEF CONFUSION OFFICER.** "Probe the edge and ask good questions," he's fond of saying.

Yahoo have their **Paranoid in Chief** (head information security guy).

Vayner Media have a **Chief Heart Officer** (HR director).

Other examples I've come across recently include **Chief Awesome Officer, Chief of Customer Happiness,** and even a **Dreams Courier** in Hong Kong.

But the gold medallist in this category must surely be Cranium Toy company. The co-founders go by the titles of **Grand Poo Bah** and the **Chief Noodler.** The CFO is **Professor Profit,** and the head of the toy business is **The Viceroy of Toy**.

"We wanted to make sure everything about our company was fun," said founder (and former Microsoft executive), Richard Tait. "So we decided to give ourselves creative job titles. Now *all* new employees we hire are empowered to develop their own special title."

They've gone on to become the fastest growing toy company in the world and won the Toy of the Year 'Oscars' more times than anyone in the past 20 years.

The secret here is to have something consistent with your company's culture, values and story. Because, as a very first impression and brand signal, it sets the tone.

And a great one (like the Paranoid in Chief) says a lot about where you come from in performing that role. You can picture it, can't you?

If you've seen, heard, got (or even dreamt up) a really great job title, I'd love to hear it.

Finally, a question for you:

What might be a better job title that gets to the heart of what you really do?

Even if you can't use it officially on your stationery, if you apply it casually, that might help reframe how YOU see your important role, and what others can rightfully expect from you in that role.

Why your office feels like a battlefield.

The expression "VUCA" started life in the US military to describe battlefield conditions. You know, much like the conditions you're finding at your office today.

VUCA stands for:

Volatile

Uncertain

Chaotic

Ambiguous.

In other words: What the F*** is Going On???

Or, strategic uncertainty as we like to politely call it in the board-room.

But to me it's all in how we frame it.

So here's my alternative take on VUCA:

Vibrant!
Unexpected!
Creative!
Adaptive!

Try being that instead. You're welcome.

Budgeting for Experimentation.

Most of us dread budgeting for next year, right? Thank God that's over for another year, is our usual feeling on getting it signed off.

May I ask (rhetorically only) how much money you set aside for "experimentation"?

That's right. How much did you set aside to try new things you or your organization have never tried before? Exercises (be they product development or marketing or workplaces changes) that have an unknown and uncertain outcome because they've never been attempted before?

Hmmm, I thought so.

How do we find the future if we're only repeating the safe and known past?

Like 3M, Google, and Gore, try to put some time and money aside to explore what's next.

Because if we are only repeating 'the sure things' they soon stop working for us, as markets and consumers and business climates rapidly change around us.

Where Will You Be Working Today?

Various studies show that 60-90% of all business ideas we have are not conceived at our desk.

But that's exactly where Industrial Age (read: Stone Age) Managers love to see their people, because they LOOK like they're working productively and she can easily control them with the big stick from there.

So ...

Where are you going to be doing your work today?

100 Better Ways to Spend Your Lunchtime.

Every now and then, a book comes a long and I think 'Doh!' why didn't I think of that?

Kaley Chu, originally from Hong Kong and working in Australia as a 'wealth advisor', was shy, felt short on confidence, and wanted to broaden her horizons.

So she hit on the idea of tapping into her LinkedIn network and inviting successful contacts for lunch.

She's now clocked up nearly 150 lunches, and has a wealth of experiences under her belt as a result. And now she's written a book about these meet-ups, which will catapult her confidence and career even further.

Now here's the thing about networking ...
There are two types of networking: Delivery-driven and Discovery-driven.

The first type is your classic networking where you're trying to 'sell' yourself or your company (to advance your own career or company).

The second type is where your job or company is not at the heart of the meeting nor discussion. It's one of the 5 core Innovation Discovery Skills.
(The others are Observation, Challenging, Experimentation, and Associative Thinking.)

Because you're looking to meet cool people doing cool stuff, you're looking to find out what's new and exciting in the world, you might even use them as a sounding board for an idea in progress. That sort of thing.

It's not a date. It's not a search for popularity or friendship. In fact, I recommend talking to more people who you are *incompatible* with or whose ideas don't sit squarely in your frame. Who knows, it might be the jolt out of confirmation bias that you need.

Kaley practiced the second type, with her work and business not on the agenda for each lunchtime chat. But her business has benefitted from mentoring from wildly successful contacts cemented, and yes some referrals to her as a result.

But mainly she's overcome the shyness she set out to conquer, and has broadened her horizons considerably.

You have around 240 available weekday lunch times each year.

How do you plan to use them better now?

Surely not by going with the same gang to the same restaurant/food court/lunch stall each day, right?

Another book you might want to read to build your confidence is Jin Jiang's Rejection Proof, in which he sets himself up for potential failure (or a slap in the face) 100 times over 100 days. Funny and inspiring stuff.

He's got tons of videos on YouTube of his experiments. I suggest starting with this one at Krispy Kreme which changed the trajectory of his life.

<u>A Sure Sign of Bad Thinking.</u>

Oh, dear!

As I was heading down a long drab corridor to find the venue of my storytelling skills workshop for a government board in Singapore quite recently, I came across this sign.

Clearly, their innovation program didn't go too well.
Some technocrat had obviously won a minor battle to rename this room.
What a negative signal to send out.

You may as well have a sign that says 'Abandon Hope All Ye Who Enter Here!'

Where's the harm in keeping something a little more inspirational and aspirational on the wall anyway?

I mean it's gotta be called something, so why not 'Innovation Room' rather than just generic 'meeting room'?

But ...

By calling a room the "Innovation" room is sort of declaring that innovation isn't or shouldn't be happening in other parts of the building, so it kind of backfires, right?

I've seen companies who use names of cities they operate in, famous practitioners and inventors in their field (ie scientists or techies), and even names of their high profile products (ie brazuca, after the World Cup soccer ball).

What are some of the best meeting room names you've seen, or can think of??? Why not change the names of the meeting rooms

in your space?

ON STRATEGIC
THINKING.

The War on Legacy Thinking.

Years ago, I attended an airline client's conference in Seattle. A great harbour-side city which was then the centre of the surging grunge music scene (remember Nirvana etc?). I also took the opportunity to drop into the Microsoft campus at Redmond, because they were also a client and we were about to launch Windows 95 for them.

What an eye-opener that was. Young stock-optioned kids in shorts pulling up in the Microsoft car park in the latest model Ferraris, Mercedes, etc (this was years before Tesla was invented). Free food in the canteen. And an open-style free-form work environment which seemed more summer camp than serious workplace.

Of course, now, all of that has become the norm in Silicon Valley and more progressive companies around the world who know how to motivate the best performance from their people.
With the conference over, I went for a poke around the city and stumbled across a fabulous old antique store in a former waterfront warehouse. What an Aladdin's cave of stuff! Right at the back left-hand corner of the shop I spotted an Underwood typewriter, a 1928 model. You know the elegantly clunky cast iron things that weight approximately the same as a Mini Minor. It was gleaming, in perfect working order, and only $65. Sold!

Typing on it, though, proved more difficult because its circular keys took some pressure to press down, and when you did, they triggered a metal swing arm with that letter on it to go crashing into the page, and then spring back, ready to be triggered again.

But at least the swing arms were not tangling. Because that problem had already been solved in 1874 by American inventor Christopher Scholes who had developed the QWERTY keyboard layout (which this Underwood typewriter had).

Now, over 140 years later, we still use the QWERTY keyboard. Long after the original problem of swinging crashing metal arms has gone away. And long after other options, such as the Dvorak keyboard which boasted an increase of 30% in productivity, have been created.

Why?

Two words: 'Legacy Thinking.'

To sum that up in one word: 'Habit.'

Legacy thinking is basically 'the way we've always done it around here'. And the sheer force of that inertia is what has

driven many design decisions, long after the reason for that thing had disappeared.

For example, broadsheet newspapers. Large, impractical, un-wieldy, especially when trying to read it on a train or plane. They were introduced in 1712 after the British government imposed taxes on newspapers based on how many pages they contained. Solution: print on larger broadsheet pages, therefore less pages, therefore less tax. But now that the tax no longer exists why do newspapers still persist in using that impractical format?

Legacy thinking.

Another example: why do modern jet planes have the main controls on the left? Because historically cavalry officers mounted horses from the left, so that their swords and legs didn't tangle. Well, that problem has clearly gone away, but the design decision still unquestioningly persists.

Legacy thinking.

Yet another example: the width of the standard gauge rail line in the USA is 4 foot 8.5 inches. Why? Because the early railways were constructed by the British. So they used the British gauge. Why were British rail lines 4 foot 8.5 inches wide? Because that's how wide the tramlines used to be. Why were the tramlines that wide? Because the people who built the trams employed machines used to build horse carriages before. And that was the width of the wheel ruts in the old roads of England. And who built those original roads? The ancient Romans about 1800 years ago.

Legacy thinking.

The examples go on for ever: Why do we have a salute? To lift your visor to be identified. Why do we shake hands with the right hand? To show we're not going to reach for our sword. Why do cars have two headlights? Because the horse carriage had two, one to light the way each side of the horse. Well, the horse has long since gone, but we still measure engines in horsepower, don't we?

You get the idea.

Legacy thinking is all around, carried forward mindlessly in many cases. Just because.

In the business world I call it 'Corporate Cargo' ... those great sand-bags of ballast that might be slowing us down, holding us back, creating drag and lag.

Take a minute now to think of what Legacy Thinking exists in your industry? In your company? In your business unit?

So is there a quick fix?

I'm not sure it's quick. But the best thing is to start resisting nostalgia. Don't remain married to ideas, solutions and practices for which the original catalyst problem has long since disappeared.

Respect **the past of your industry and your company.**

But don't *revere* **it.**

By revering it, we accept too many of the built-in assumptions and that just adds to our baggage.
Oh, and why are you wearing that tie? You do know that they were invented back in the 17th century, and were first used to identify Croatian mercenaries fighting for King Louis X111? Well, that war is long since over, my friends.

But -- whether you are in Seattle, Shanghai, Singapore or Sydney -- the war on Legacy Thinking must start today. Smells like teen spirit to me.

What Won't You Do Today?

Our life is often dominated by 'to do' lists, which run to several pages.

We chase the 'urgent' things often at the expense of the 'important' things to do.

Until finally the 'important' things also become 'urgent'.

We stumble from one over-crowded workday to another. And so it goes ...

I've watched with interest the rise and rise of the social phenomenon of Marie Kondo (you know, the de-clutter queen).

And I thought, How can we apply the same principal to our business?

Sadly we can't just stop doing *all* the things that don't spark joy around the office (otherwise there might be very little left to do).

But what we can do is introduce the Triple Ex Innovation Framework. (I call it that because if it was the XXX Innovation Framework, well, HR might have some questions.)

Think of it as three tidy Marie Kondo-approved boxes:
Exploit
Extinguish
Explore

Exploit: keep on making the most of the things that are making us money. Repeat your winners! They will finance your future.

Extinguish: this is the Marie Kondo box. Get rid of products which are unprofitable, solutions which don't suit your core competencies, people who are not forward-compatible with your progressive values, etc. Kill, kill, kill.

Explore: now you will find you have freed up resources (people, money, etc) from your 'Extinguish' exercise which can be re-allocated more effectively and productively. Pump some back into your 'Exploit' activities, and importantly pump some into exploring innovative and market-delighting new products, solutions, revenue streams, energizing talent hires, and so on.

Among authors and creatives there's a term we use a lot: "Kill your darlings!" Meaning, don't get so attached to an idea or a character that they get in the way of the story, or you go ahead with an idea because you love it, and not because it's a great and relevant idea for the market.

So, put on the kettle, and focus on that 'Extinguish' box over the next few days. Make a list of things you will kill in your organisation. Processes that are holding you back, products or practices that are dragging you down, middle managers thieving too much oxygen.

Ask yourself: "What WON'T I do today?"
Then take great delight in killing them.
That should spark some joy.

(Tip: read 'The 3 Box Solution' by Vijay Govindarajan.)

Cathedral Thinking. What It Is and Why We Need More of it Now.

My partner, who has lived in France before, awoke me one morning with images of the Notre Dame Cathedral ablaze. I'm sure you've seen the images, too.

Over 700 years of history -- and 200 years of painstaking innovation and craftsmanship -- up in smoke.

Built on a long-term artistic and engineering vision which long outlived its originators, and draws millions to its stunning beauty centuries later.

Which only served to highlight to me what an instant-gratification world we now live in ... a world fixated by the short term.

We're increasingly exhorted to live in the moment, *this* moment.

Our bosses want results by 5pm Friday.

Our companies want better performance this month.

Wall St wants results this quarter. Or else.

Politicians in many countries have only a 3-year horizon to map out and enact.

But what comes *after* that?

There is another perspective we can take, and it was recently brought to my attention by my former client, fellow author, and all-round adventurous human being, Rick Antonson.

Formerly the President & CEO of Tourism Vancouver, he has become an evangelist for "cathedral thinking."

Essentially it is something with a far-reaching vision, and long-term implementation. (You know, exactly the sort of things which are *not* in your KPIs.)

But it's the sort of approach with which we can transcend ordinary everyday thinking and behaviours in our personal and professional lives. The sort of thing which can help you and your company find a more meaningful true north purpose.

Take 9 minutes out of your busy day now, grab a cup of tea or coffee, and enjoy this wonderful TEDx talk by Rick on "cathedral thinking." And watch how he delivers his message with such an enviable measured and authentic tone.

<u>Ignoring the red flags.</u>

When the first commercial automobile was launched, it rolled down the street at around 10 km/h, with a man walking ahead of it waving a red flag to ensure people were warned about this new menace that was replacing the horse and cart on the roads.

Amazingly, though, accidents did happen, and people were actually run over by this new phenomenon, the motorcar. Didn't see it coming, or didn't move fast enough to get out of the way.

In business, especially in a big successful corporation, we are terribly bad at seeing or paying attention to red flags.
Big warning signs. Often clear as day to others, but not to us.

One of my favourite examples is Blockbuster, the video rental chain. At its peak, it employed 84,000 people, and was one of the most valuable and recognizable brands on the planet, with revenues of over $3.2 bn.

In 1997, the Silicon Valley veteran Reed Hastings founded Netflix, partly out of frustration after being fined $40 in late fees by

Blockbuster for returning "Apollo 13" late.

This led to a wonderful series of creative challenging by Hastings who set about disrupting the whole video rental value chain. The main assumption that was challenged was the whole 'video rental' bit.

But here's the thing ...

In 2012, HBR interviewed the CEO of Blockbuster, Michael Kelly. When asked about Netflix his somewhat complacent and arrogant reply was: "Haha, *those* guys! They're not even on our radar."

Within two years, Blockbuster had filed for bankruptcy.

Netflix is now worth $150 BILLION!

So why don't we see red flags?

A couple of reasons. They are rarely big red things that are waving, or flashing neon signs, unfortunately. They typically start as feint signals. Something that's there in the market, but easy to gloss over if you're not paying close attention. Until it grows, and grows ...

Secondly, they might be clear, as Netflix probably might have been, but then wilful blindness kicks in. We *choose* to ignore it. We hope it's going to go away. We choose to believe that seismic shift won't happen in *our* industry. We believe we're too big to fail. After all, we're one of the world's leading brands, right?

Yup! So were Kodak, Pan Am, Borders ...

Question for you to ponder over a cup of coffee with your team:
What are the red flags in your business or industry that you're not seeing (or choosing not to see) today? And what are you going to do about it?

And one for the disruptors:
What are you doing so differently that it should be a red flag to your competitors and industry model?

My 9 word business plan.

I wondered whether I should share my business plan for 2019 with you or not? I finally decided: yes.
So here it is...

"Make my *next* event the most *impactful* one ever."

All 9 words of it. And it's exactly the same as my business plan for 2016, 2017, 2018.
As a trainer, speaker and facilitator, if I can keep on hitting that, it means the lessons are being learned, the transformations are being made, and the experience is rich and meaningful. Then the word of mouth takes care of itself. And my tribe grows. 82% of my workload is Fortune 500 clients coming back for more.

Which is why I limit myself to only 80 workshop face-days per year. To keep me mentally and physically fresh. With enough time in between to tweak the material till the last minute -- and even as a workshop runs sometimes -- to best serve those who've invested their valuable time, emotion, (and money) to be in the room.

Business plans are an interesting thing.

Have a look at this research on Inc 500 companies:

12% conducted formal market research before launch

40% wrote formal business plans

(of those, 2/3 ditched them later!)

(Source: Crazy is a Compliment, Rottenberg)

Even more interesting is that the founders of Microsoft, Pixar and Starbucks never wrote a business plan. The founders of Intel did. It was only 161 words long and 'adn' was spelt wrongly!

Bill Sahlman, entrepreneurial finance guru from Harvard Business School tells us:

> **"Business plans rank no higher than 2 (out of 10)**
> **as a predictor of a new venture's success.**
> **Smart businesses adapt and change."**

So what does your business plan for the Year of the Rat look like?

Is it 100 pages long? Is it full of empty but important sounding buzzwords? What are you *really* trying to achieve this year? What's going to make the most impact? Focus on *that*.

Turn that into a 9-word business plan now.

And stick it above your workspace where you can see it every day.

We need a new word for Disruption.

Don't get me wrong. I'm a huge fan of the late Dr Clayton Christensen's work. Especially his game-changing book "Innovator's Dilemma."

But I have a bone to pick with him because with the release of that title in 1997 he hijacked the word "disruptive innovation" and has sent a generation of corporate cubicle jockeys searching vainly in the wrong direction.
(Never mind that he actually coined the phrase in the first place.)

This was highlighted when I ran a workshop in Shanghai on Disruptive Thinking for a sportswear brand whose product you are very likely to be wearing somewhere on your body at this very moment.

We spent quite a bit of time up-front getting aligned on what disruption is ... and isn't.

By Christensen's definition it's the ongoing migration to the northeast quadrant of more bells and whistles, greater complexity, higher price, etc. Which creates a vacuum in the southwest quadrant for someone to bring in a more basic, functional, possibly stripped-down version of your thing that performs roughly the same job at a lower price.

Hence new market entrants appear, build a following, and start gradually swimming upstream after you and gobbling up your market. You know, as in "disrupting" you and spoiling your day, if not your whole financial quarter. I get it.

But ...

The problem is this.

What word do we have to describe those innovations that jump into the market and completely turn the world upside down? You know, guys like AirBNB, Uber, Netflix.

That's truly disruptive to me because it fits the dictionary definition (thanks, Cambridge) such as "causing trouble and therefore stopping something from continuing as usual."

I'm working with a broadcasting company in Malaysia that has been completely broadsided by Netflix. That disruption has got nothing to do with lower prices, less functionality or being stripped down. In fact it's the opposite. But the consumer delight and enhanced entertainment experience of Netflix is apparently worth paying for.

Yes, we can call these step innovations or platform innovations. But those terms don't nearly have the punk energy to capture the anarchy, the gung-ho creativity, and the market mayhem that's unleashed by these sorts of players.

The other problem is of course overuse of the word "disruptive." Very few things truly are that extreme to warrant it. And some more conservative types (such as the consumer goods industry) confuse a 1% marginal gain for being disruptive, because in their world that's considered really moving the needle. It's a good day's work, but it's NOT really disruptive.

Even the king of disruption, Elon Musk -- not known for treading lightly on anything -- treads lightly with this word.

"I don't actually like to disrupt, that sounds ... Disruptive! I am much more inclined to say, How can we make things better?"

So maybe we need a whole new word? Radical Innovation, perhaps.

What are YOUR suggestions?

Would love to hear them, because I'd like us all to move to a greater common understanding of what disruptive innovation is. Anyway, thanks Dr Christensen, for starting the conversation in the first place. Your book was really ... um ... radical.

Response: I put forward the idea that we needed a new word for 'disruptive' innovation. Well, some readers came forward with tons of interesting alternatives:

Chris in Thailand: 'Transformative innovation.'

James in New Zealand: 'Left of Centre Profit Derivation.'

A different Chris in Thailand: 'Tsunovation ... as in a tidal shift.'

Kevin in Queensland: 'Pragmatic Disruption.'

Sandy in Australia: 'Neoteric.'

Personally I love the power of the tidal shift most. Perhaps Seismic Shift?

ON CUSTOMER-CENTRICITY.

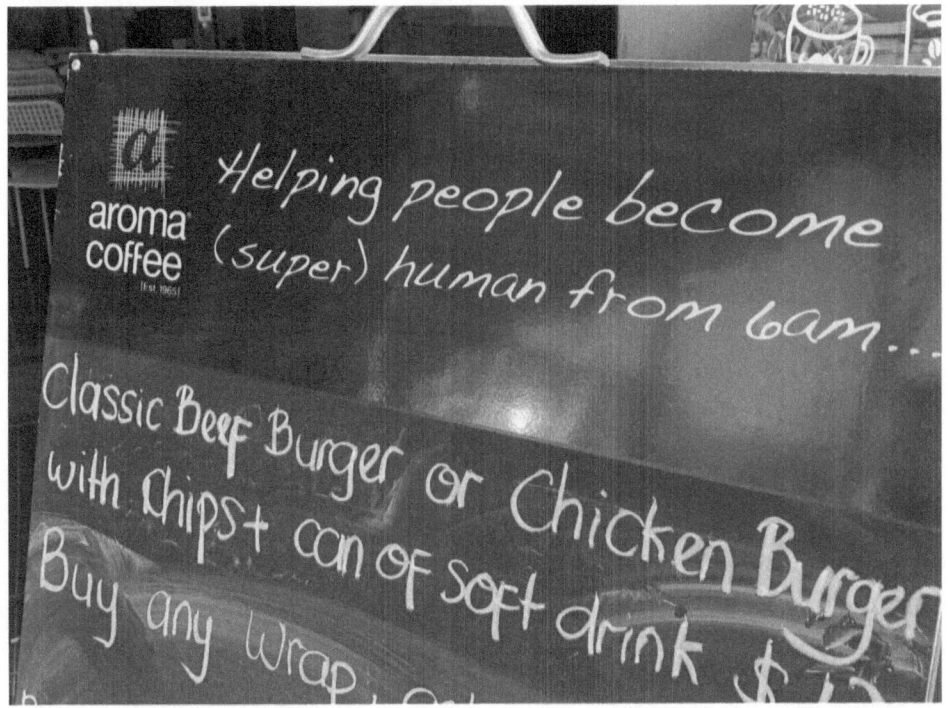

Those two lines at the top are loaded with value and benefit.

More importantly they tell us that the owner knows exactly what business she's in.

She doesn't just sell coffee. Everybody does that.

Instead her product, service, and experience help to magically transform you from Early Morning Zombie You, into a More Awake Human You, into totally Super Human You so you can go and kick ass.

It's called benefit laddering, or as I recently heard it called: 'Super-Claiming'.

What's the ultimate emotional benefit of the benefit?

So, question for you to think about as you enjoy your coffee this morning:

What business are you *really*, Really, REALLY in?

<u>What Empathy Looks Like...</u>

Mr Kwan turned up within 3 minutes of me confirming my Grab ride.

"Good morning, sir," the 60-something Singaporean gent sang as he helped me load my signature yellow suitcase.

"Good morning, boss." (I call everyone "boss" at first if I don't know their name.)
As we got into the car, he immediately switched from a Mandarin talk station -- obviously his favourite -- to an English music station.

After a couple of minutes he asked: "Air temperature ok for you, sir?"

Yes, everything is fine thanks.

As we passed through the East Coast a really good song came on the radio and I started tapping the beat on my leg. With a quick glance in the mirror he sensed my joy and turned up the volume for me. And the hits kept coming so the volume stayed up.

Until just before Changi Airport. My phone rang. Without missing a beat he lowered the music, fading out like a seasoned radio DJ.

At the airport he insisted on helping me with my bag again, even though he was a good 15 years older and 20 kg lighter than me.

I paid my fare, adding a few bucks tip: "Mr Kwan, when you stop for a break, please buy yourself a coffee. And you can put it back on to Mandarin now." He grinned widely.

This is what empathy looks like in action. Yes it sounds like just a good service story, but that's the thing: whether he knew it or not, Mr Kwan was curating a frictionless experience for me, based on empathy. He knows the ride is about me, not about him, although it's *his* office, and he's driving in it all day.

This resulted in better service, which resulted in a happy customer, which resulted in a good review, a good tip, and a more productive flight home for me because I felt all was well in the modern trust economy.

Empathy doesn't announce itself. It just listens, observes and adjusts the sails according to that feedback loop.
Whether between individuals, a brand or a business.

How can you curate a better experience for your customers today?

Under Promise, Over Deliver.

I was served this sandwich on Air Asia recently.

Worst. Sandwich. Ever.

Even if it wasn't over-processed mass-produced nonsense posing as ham and cheese, it was *NEVER* going to live up to the hyperbole on the package ...

Under promise. Over deliver.
Not the other way round.

How could you over-deliver on a customer or client's expect-

ations today? Go and do that thing.

Innovative Leadership Starts With This Skill.

As I walk back from the gym each morning, I turn the corner into our little street, and I see two big black noses sticking through our garden fence. It's our two Labradors, Schofield (named after the main character in Prison Break) and Scarlett (named after Scarlett Johansson).

Noses is how dogs make sense of their world.

Did you know they have up to 300 million olfactory receptors in their noses, compared to a mere six million in us humans? That's 50 times more smelling potential, and the part of their brain devoted to crunching smells is proportionally large, being at least 40 times as large as ours.

Growing up in the countries like Zimbabwe, South Africa and Australia, I was surrounded by snakes (often literally) and they make sense of the world by smelling with their tongues, flicking them out to pick up tiny chemical particles in the air.

So the question is this:

How do you and your company make sense of your world? What's your nose and tongue in the customer's or consumer's market? How do you pick up trends, early warning signals?

Developing your observation and empathy skills is a great way to do this, which is why Design Thinking methodology (which starts with these skills) can help in shaping your innovation directions. We have to read the early smoke signals before they becoming raging fires and burning platforms.

So stick your nose into someone's business today if you want to innovate better.

Is Your Business Over-Promising?

I was recently wondering through Palo Alto, in Silicon Valley, trying to soak in the Creative Kool-Aid. There was so much cool stuff to absorb, from the cloistered courtyards of Stanford University, to a Beam store (with absolutely no human shop assistants) selling telepresence equipment, to burger and coffee stores promising world-changing experiences for customers and employees alike.

But what caught my eye most was this tradesman's truck.

Can you imagine why?

That's right ... the story disconnect.

He's selling "STUNNING" sign-writing services, and yet his very own vehicle -- pardon the pun -- is anything but stunning.

In fact, to me it looks like a failed apprentice's practice project. Leaving the impression that if that's the best he can do for himself, gee, he's probably not the best guy to be doing the work for us.

Here's a question for you.

Where's the story disconnect in YOUR business or brand? What brand signal are you sending out that is actually sending the opposite message to customers and staff?

Identify it, and fix it quickly.

(If you need help, we use the 6Ps Framework to identify hundreds of 'communication surfaces' that are sending signals that you are probably not even aware of -- including one that 98% of businesses like yours miss). The 6Ps of innovation are: Product, Process, Promotion, Premises, People, Purpose.

ON PEAK PERFORMANCE.

Something I'll Never Ever Do Again.

Allow me to tell you about a week in my life which happened a little while back ...

On the Sunday, I flew to KL to run a Digital Content Creation full-day workshop for producers and creatives at **Astro**, Malaysia's largest TV & Radio broadcaster on the Monday. I then raced to the airport to jump a flight to Bangkok.

On the Tuesday, I ran a full day Storytelling workshop for **GTA**, one of the world's biggest players in the B2B travel and tourism space. (This was a follow up to a 3-day **global #YourStory** Conference I'd hosted for them earlier.)

On the Wednesday I did a half-day webinar with the APAC leadership team from **COACH** luxury goods. Then off to the airport to fly to Shanghai.

Thursday and Friday I ran a 2-day Design Thinking forum for the Innovation department at **Intel**.

On the Sunday, I flew to Hong Kong to run a full-day POP THINK disruptive thinking workshop for **Adidas** (who I work with in 15 markets around Asia).

I then flew home, and collapsed like a starfish on my bed, absolutely mentally and physically spent. The adrenaline and caffeine withdrew from my body over the course of the next few days, as I decompressed and reflected on the previous week.

8 days, 6 workshops, 4 countries.

It was exciting, thrilling, challenging to work with so many differently great minds. Satisfying to feel that my skills work was pushing the right buttons with clients, and I was fully booked. And it was a wildly profitable week. Woohoo!

But ... but I resolved to myself to NEVER EVER DO THAT AGAIN.

Why not?

44 hours of thinking on my feet that week.

Each workshop takes a lot of preparation, customizing as best as I can to who's in the room and what they need from me to help them fly higher. Each workshop also requires a lot of physical and mental energy. So I need to be mentally and physically fresh to give my best performance and inspire others.

How can someone who drags his weary ass into the room be an inspiration? I have to live and breathe my message.

So I put in place a quota system: a limit of no more than 10 face days per month. And a maximum of 8 months per year. So there's only 80 live events on offer each year. Maximum. Because if I was greedy and went for more, word would soon get around that I wasn't giving everything to each event. I would just become a hack trainer.

If I made a word cloud of all the evaluations, "PASSION" and "ENERGY" are the two that would probably pop the loudest.

And if I didn't live up to that, my word of mouth referrals would soon dry up (82% of my work is happy customers coming back for more).

You can't stand out unless you know what you stand for. And

that's something I would never dare compromise.

So, what would YOU never do again in order to improve your performance at work?

Because sometimes it's what we DON'T or WON'T DO which says the most about us.

The Last 10%.

Just about everyone can perform the first 80% of any job assigned to them.

That's the easy part. (And it's entry-level table stakes by the way).

Think of painting a large wall. A relative novice can cover most of the middle section in paint.

The next 10% of any job becomes harder. Greater detail, more granularity and skill needed.

The hardest part comes when you get to the edges and the corners.

The final 10%.

This is where more eye for detail, care, effort, hard work, expertise, is required.

So here's the thing:

What if we put 90% of our effort into the last 10% of the job, the proposal, the product development, the manufacturing?

Because those are the little details, touches and flourishes your customers will notice most.

They'll notice if you didn't even attempt the fine brushwork. They'll notice if you didn't go right up to the corner evenly. They'll notice if you went over the lines.

They'll notice if you think you can get away with "good enough" because "good enough" is not good enough anymore.

The Last Mile is not very crowded, because many can't be bothered to go all that way.

And if you don't think the small things don't matter, consider the full stop:

It may not seem much.

But it could be the difference between being No One and No.1.

Intermittent Thinking.

We've got it all wrong, folks!

The research shows that there is NO correlation between the hours you put in and how much *effective* output you create. In fact, the opposite is often true.

Because we get fatigued, we achieve 'cognitive backlog' (meaning your head's full). And so we start turning in half-baked stuff, with careless sloppy errors and oversights.

Because we are humans and our brains cannot simply be switched on to full turbo-thrusting Power Thinking mode and sustain it for 8 hours a day (or more, especially our friends in South Korea and Japan). We get fried.

And I've seen it often walking through clients' offices ...

Brain-dead Zombies sitting at their computers, pretending to be productive long into the night, until they see their boss leave.

What's the solution?

Intermittent Fasting seems to be all the rage these days. (The 5:2

Diet in particular seems popular with many) so might Intermittent *Thinking* be the way forward?

Well, there's good science for why we should do it ...

Ever wonder why TED talks are only 20 minutes long?
Ever wonder why the Finnish school system (regarded the best in the world by many educators) gives kids a 15-minute break after each 45-minute lesson?
Ever wonder why the world's most successful and prolific creative artists work far less than 8 hours per day?

We need to refresh, change 'Brain Shape' (the chemical settings involved in our attention, engagement, learning, etc), then go back to it again. *Intermittently.*

For those of you who follow cricket, you'll know that Steve Smith, the great Australian batsman, scored two centuries (score of over 100 runs) in a match against England in 2019.

It is estimated that he is only fully switched on to concentration mode for around 7.5 minutes in that period to reach a typical century. Because concentration is a rare commodity. The rest of the time he's unfocussed, fidgeting, deliberately distracting himself.

That way, he's absolutely focussed when he needs to be: when the bowler starts his run in to deliver the next ball.
Seems counter-intuitive, but he's got the runs on the board, literally.

How might you apply this knowledge to your day's work for better performance and output?

Understand your brainpower and neuro-biology for a start. For most people on average biorhythm you have two peak cognitive periods in the day. 10am - 12 noon, then 3 - 5pm. Assign these windows for your serious thinking and more creative tasks.

Within that 2-hour window, you can consider using the Pomodoro Technique. This methodology assigns 25 minutes to each task before you take a short break (step away from your desk, walk around, grab a coffee, play social media, etc). Anything to change your Brain Shape. Fill this slot with 4 x Pomodoros before you take a 'serious' break.

So your new workday might be a 2:5. Two hours of full-on focus, and five hours of other stuff with its usual interruptions and distractions. Later you might want to step it up to 4:3.

Sound like something you might want to try?
There's a cool app Pomodoro Tracker which can help you stay on task when you should be, and stepping away from it when you need to.

And if you want to deep-dive more into this, why not read Two Awesome Hours. I haven't read this book yet, but from the blurb I understand Josh Davis, PhD, is saying the same thing as I am although he's not clear on why he chose 2 hours.

Good luck in fitting this to your work life for a more efficient and effective you.

At least, take a break, and think about it.

Curiosity.

Former CEO, AG Lafley, tripled the innovation success of P&G under his watch.

In short he moved a successful company from having 10 x billion-dollar brands to having 24 x billion-dollar brands.

While there were many factors driving this, I love the fact that he had one abiding question running through his mind at the time:

"What will I decide to be *curious* about on Monday morning?"

If you start the week on a positive, curious and creative note, hopefully that'll set the tone for the next 5 days.

Extrapolated, if everyone on your team is thinking this way, it's a fast-track shortcut to a curious organization.

Coffee, Sex and Chocolate.

Three of my favourite things (though not necessarily in that order).

Now I've got your attention -- and why I want to bring your attention to these 3 things -- is that they might be among the best things to help your creative thinking according to a number of university research studies I've come across.

Really? How? Why?

What they all have in common is something dear to my heart (well head actually) as someone with a psychology background.

They are all excellent ways to fire the neurotransmitter dopamine into your system.

Think of it as lubricating your brain.

So that you are able to join dots from all that precious knowledge, information, and experiences stored all over your brain. Left and right, top and bottom, back and front.

Dopamine helps you to reach into those filing cabinets and facilitate a creative connection, the synaptic spark which leads to the AHA! moment.

1. With chocolate, make sure it's dark chocolate, 70% cocoa or above. That way you avoid the sugar spike crash of milk chocolate, which would negate the effect.

2. Coffee. Most research points to between 2-5 cups a day as being a good amount to fire up creative benefit. If I have more than 2 cups of coffee my brain is too buzzed and I lose concentration and clarity. Find your sweet spot and know your limit of caffeine.

Of these, dark chocolate is better (no sugar crash) and is proving itself to be the secret weapon of creative people. I've become an evangelist for the stuff. That's why I often dish it out as prizes in workshops.

3. Sex. A 'satisfying' session will also release a huge surge of feel-good chemicals (including dopamine) into your brain, laying the conditions for clearer creative thinking.

Fun team question: how would you rank those three items from favourite to least favourite?

I hope you enjoy these creative thinking hacks responsibly (and appropriately, otherwise HR is going to hound me).

3 Reasons Why Standing and Walking is Good For Your Creativity.

Creativity loves movement.

And it especially rewards *STANDING UP*.

Here's 3 proven reasons to stand:

1. Hold a standing meeting. Your meetings will be over quicker, about **25% shorter** according to the research I've seen. And because you're not slouched in that comfy chair, you might even think a little bit sharper because ...

2. When you stand up, within 60 seconds you'll have about **15% more oxygen-rich blood to fuel your brain**. So you WILL actually be thinking sharper.

3. Better still, **hold a walking meeting**. Grab your 2 or 3 colleagues and a cup of coffee and walk around the office instead of being inside the constricting space of your meeting room. Especially if you've got a nice park nearby, or at least some trees, the boost from unstructured nature will ensure you have up to a **60% increase in creative thinking power** at your disposal.

It worked for Steve Jobs, and it works for Mark Zuckerberg, Beth Comstock (CMO of GE), and many others.

I urge you to try it today.

And then make it your new habit.

Cool, huh?

PS: The research on stand-up desks (which I know some of you use) is so far scientifically inconclusive so I've not included it here. But, if it works for YOU, then do it.

Are You Just a Meat Machine?

I just finished reading Man Out of Time, a biography of Nikolai Tesla by Margaret Cheney.

The main thing that struck me was how the concepts and ideas he was envisaging 100 years ago, are the big problems the cutting-edge start-ups in Silicon Valley are trying to solve today.

A key concept he often riffed on was that of human workers as a "meat machine".

Corporate cannon fodder who offered no discernible added-value by their involvement in the process.

Worker bees who could easily be replaced by a machine.

If only we could make a machine smart.

And now we have.

It's called Artificial Intelligence. #AI.

And so we come to the death of the middleman -- any person who is simply a mailman in a process.

Carry a paper from A to B? No value. We can do that digitally.

Bookstores with staff that no nothing about the genres, authors, titles they sell? No value. We can do that digitally.

Front-line service staff who offer no personalised humanity? No value. We can do that digitally.

Trainers who are not deep-dive experts in articulating their subject matter in an engaging way? No value. We can do that digitally.

So look around you.

Who are the "mailmen" on your team?

It's time to save their livelihoods by up-skilling them for the future ... give them some critical thinking skills, some creative ability to think out of the box (God, I hate that expression!), and some presentation and persuasion skills to function in the new economy.

Otherwise they are just a "meat machine" headed to the butchery. You have been warned by Tesla 100 years ago, and I'm reminding you now. Because it's become urgent.

Are You Open to New Ideas?

My friend, David in Shanghai, recently told me an interesting story.

He'd asked his team what they did for lunch.
Their response was "The usual place," with a sort of bored shrug.

"Hey, did you know there's a really great Mexican restaurant, just behind, about 50 metres round the corner. Why don't you try that?"
"Maybe we won't like it."
"How do you know if you've never tried Mexican food before? Maybe you *will* like it."

And so of course the next day, the team was back at the usual place, eating the same lunch again.

Now here's the thing ...
Creative people say YES to more things, more often.

They are always OPEN to new experiences.

And "openness" (as we call it in psychology) is one of the big 5 personality traits that shows up strongly in creatives.

Because new sights, sounds, flavours, people, experiences, etc, are the raw material for inspiration, insights and ideas.

It's where creativity really comes from.

So, how OPEN are YOU?

Take this free 10 minute test here or search online for an 'openness test'

And next time someone suggests an art exhibition, a movie, a band, an activity, a holiday destination that may not fit your current preference, just say YES.

It might open a whole new world to you.

Like it or not, that's how we grow.

Authenticity and You.

In this world of fake news, alternative facts and greater disingenuous behaviour, people are looking to weed out the frauds.

Their 'bullshit detectors' are in overdrive, and their filters are up. So we need to drop the mask and be our own authentic selves – hiding behind nothing and with nothing to hide.

Because authentic = trustworthy.

This little rhyme by the incomparable Dr Seuss says far more about being authentic than I possibly could tell you ...

"Today you are You, that is truer than true.

There is no one alive who is Youer than You."

So stop trying to be some perfect cookie-cutter corporate automaton.

Be real. Stay real.

ON CREATIVE CONFIDENCE & FEAR OF FAILURE.

Happy Accidents.

One day, a roadside oyster vendor in Guangzhou, Lee Kum Sheung, was boiling a pot of oysters. He was laughing and joking with some of his regular customers, got carried away, and forgot to take the oysters out of the boiling pot.

He finally lifted the lid, only to see an ugly brown gooey mass of burned bi-valves at the bottom. But the aroma was quite striking and not unpleasant. He dipped his finger in, and gave it a little lick. Hmmm, not bad. His friends gathered round, curiously.

So Kum Sheung dished up some of the sauce to his customers. Hmmm, not bad at all. In fact, very good, Mr Lee!

From then on they started demanding his burnt oyster sauce to flavour other meals and dishes.

And the sauce took on a life of its own.

He bottled it, and applied a colourful label: 'Lee Kum Kee Oyster

Sauce.'

That event happened 130 years ago, and the Lee family has turned that happy accident into a $15 billion fortune.

There is a great lesson to be learned here ...

We must be open to stumbling across solutions that we hadn't intended in our search for innovation. Experiments will go wrong, but it's what we take away from them that defines our learning and growth potential.

History is littered with similar serendipitous "happy accidents". Other products that were accidentally discovered include:

The microwave oven (trying to create an avionics radar)

Chewing gum (trying to improve rubber for car tyres)

The slinky toy (trying to improve car suspension)

Viagra (trying to create blood pressure medication)

Penicillin (trying to study something in petri dish)

The Post-it note (trying to create an adhesive)

Etc, etc, etc.

So we may not always get what we want, but we must remain alert to something even bigger and better than we had in mind in the first place.

More instructionally, Charles Lee, one of the siblings helming the business now, has shown himself to be a great entrepreneur who displays enviable traits of risk-taking. In the name of speed and agility he is comfortable at the 60-70% level of 'perfection' to green-light an idea.

(I've done work with LKK subsidiaries and staff have confirmed it.)

For an apparently conservative Chinese family business in particular this is especially admirable, being equal to the US Army's 'Fog of War' GO level of 70% certainty.

Because Charlie knows if he waits for 100% perfection before shipping, the market opportunity would pass him by.

Or, in the case of his great-grandfather, he might've thrown out the whole batch of over-cooked oysters and started again, licking his wounds rather than his fingers.

Back on your Bike.

This was Marc Marquez on Friday 4 October 2019 ...
and below is Marc Marquez less than 48 hours later ...

So, what happened in between?

Two words: Learning Moments.

I rode over 2200km with some friends to Buriram, in the remote reaches of eastern Thailand, to watch the MotoGP for the first time. I was expecting to learn and write about speed as a competitive weapon in your business. Instead, I find myself writing about managing fear of failure.

This was triggered by the news of a horrific crash in training on Friday (just after the massive rains cleared up), as World Champion Marquez lost his handling on Turn 7. He somersaulted off the track and lay prone on all fours as the crowd anxiously held its breath.

He was later taken by ambulance to the local hospital for MRI scans.

Would he be OK? Would he be competing again for all the fans this weekend?

Hell yeah!

"When you crash at 350km/h you only think of standing up again,"
the 7-time world champion tells us. "No one likes to crash."

Saturday dawned, and Marquez was champing at the bit to get back on the bike, and clinch another pole position from the qualifying rounds that day.

It was great to see the blur of his orange-and-red bike and racing suit roaring down the straight past me at nearly 355km/h again. So, what was he thinking?

"The first rival is ourselves, there are no friends on the track, you must be selfish and have no limits."

But then: disaster again! He crashed out on Turn 5, sliding off the track on to the gravel. Would he be able to back-up after a second crash in only 2 days?

Hell yeah!

Sunday's MotoGP main event arrived and he rode what many considered to be the ride of his life, trailing in second for the most part before some sneaky, daring, and outrageous riding skills saw him take the chequered flag by just 0.171 of a second.

He became an 8-time world champion in the process.

So what can we learn as creative leaders about this remarkable performance?

I believe he learned where the edge of his best performance was. And that edge was in the micro-moments just before he lost control and crashed both times. He knew what he, his Honda, and his team were capable of. He knew the extreme he could push himself and his machine too. And in the race he did *exactly* that. To perfection.

Lesser people might have lost their nerve on the Friday, at the first crash. You know what it's like when a product launch doesn't go as planned? We get dispirited, right? Others might've given up after the second crash, thinking to themselves these are not the right market conditions for success. But he was learning, learning, learning.

Plus he had the balls to get back on the bike -- mentally and physically undaunted -- and apply those learnings for a determined and glorious win.

So, what are you afraid of today? What's holding you back from your best performance at work and in life? Go and find your edges. What does extreme marketing look like? What does extreme process speed look like? What does extreme hiring look like?

Now go and perform to just within those limits. Good luck, and we'll see you on the winner's podium.

3 Quick Ways to Improve Your Creative Confidence.

I'm sure you are full of good ideas, right?

But how often do we find that when it comes to *that* meeting, that brainstorm session, at the last minute we decide not to put up our hand and say it.

Why?

Because we think our colleagues will think our idea is crazy.

(Guess what? Every game-changing idea starts out being seen as "crazy" because it doesn't fit the current mould)

Because we think our colleagues will think we are stupid.
(Guess what? Even the world's most successful creative people such as Edison, Einstein, Picasso, Jobs, Branson, had a failure rate of around 90%.)

Because we think our idea sucks.

(Guess what? Your idea WILL suck if you don't share it.

An idea not shared has ZERO value. Besides someone else might see how to build on to your idea to make it even better. So even the glimmer of an idea could be a potential stepping-stone or building block to insights and ideas for them.)

Especially in Asian cultures where there is a lot more shyness, fear of "social risk" (losing face), and general cultural complexity about suggesting creative ideas, here are 3 simple phrases to help YOU gain more creative confidence.
Try using these 3 phrases:
"This is only an idea ..."
"This may sound crazy, but ..."
"This might be the idea that leads to the idea ..."

They act as a sort of defence mechanism for the person making the suggestion, giving you a safety net, and something to hide behind if you need it.

Try them. Today. Because without creative confidence you're not unleashing your full value on the world.

ON CREATIVE THINKING & PROBLEM SOLVING.

What's your Handy Hammer?

A few years back I started experiencing excruciating pain in my right shoulder. It rapidly got worse and worse over a couple of months to the point that I could not move my arm enough to un-button my own shirt without causing little tears of pain.

It was at that point -- being a stubborn kind of guy -- I finally relented and went to see a doctor. We'll call him Doctor A, an ortho-paedic surgeon.

After a cursory inspection, in which he asked a couple of questions about my sport and gym habits, and manoeuvred my arm around in [expletive-laden] wide circles, he concluded I needed surgery. "When are you available for that?" he said consulting his calendar.

Huh?

This was all a bit sudden for me. I wasn't ready to go under the knife yet. So he showed me a video of a baseball pitcher throwing the ball. I was never going to be first-draft pitcher for the New York Yankees anyway, so I didn't really see the relevance of that as proof of my predicament. "Lie down on the bed, we're going to operate now," seemed to be his message.

So he then sent me for a wildly expensive MRI scan. As he viewed it on his monitor, he nodded his head sagely: "Yes, yes, we must operate. When can you come for the operation?"

I explained I had a busy travel schedule, but in any case was there no alternative to major reconstructive surgery? "No, no, come on, lie down." (I was by now getting the feeling he was already dreaming of his next holiday in the Maldives with the proceeds of my operation.)

He wrote down his professional diagnosis, and I again asked him if there was no other approach than surgery to explore a solution. He gave me a withering glance as though to say, "Look at my certificate on the wall, I've been doing this for 20 years, now please lie down on the bed so we can chop your shoulder apart."

What I did next was this: I took his diagnosis, and Googled it, which is what you should *never* do because then usually you are convinced that you are going to die within days from flesh-eating microbes which have crawled into your ear and are now chewing their way to the centre of your cranium.

But ...

In this case, the Google search revealed that in at least one third of cases, relief could come in the form of a single cortisone injection (for the shoulder, not the brain-eating bugs).

So I went to another hospital and consulted Doctor B. I explained to him the results of the MRI and the diagnosis. He listened care-fully, nodded sagely, and gently moved my right arm in painful arcs. "Are you a swimmer?" Yes, until recently swimming 1 to 2 kilometres before breakfast was part of my daily routine. "This is also known as 'swimmer's shoulder'," he said. Oh! So? "You could try reduce the pressure on the tendon, maybe lose some weight." We discussed my dietary intake.

He was not recommending surgery yet, he was exploring other less radical options from the solution field first.
So I asked him about the cortisone injections I'd read about. "Yes, they can be helpful, but usually only for 3 months at a time. We can try that if you like?" He jabbed two syringes into me, one into the joint socket and the other into the shoulder.

"How soon before I feel any benefit?" I asked him.

He grabbed my arm and swung it around in a full circle.
I felt no pain. Relief was immediate. I buttoned my own shirt back up, and left. "Don't forget, try to lose some weight," he repeated and wished me well.

Three months later, the familiar twinges of pain started recur-ring, then disappeared just as suddenly. And since then I've not had a moment's pain in it. That was 9 years ago now.

So what can we learn from this?

It's called 'THE HANDY HAMMER'.

Sometimes the more deeply experienced and specialised we be-come in business, the more we develop narrower views on what the solution is. And with more experience that often becomes even narrower, until we can only think of one solution.

Psychologist Abraham Maslow said it best: "If all you have is a hammer, everything looks like a nail."

And that's the Handy Hammer. Your Go-To Tool. Doctor A's handy hammer was his scalpel. He was trained to use that, and he possibly used it well. But it shut down his ability to think more holistically of my problem and possible solutions.

As a CEO (and hello to our valued CEO readers) your handy hammer to increase profits might be "cost reduction."

As a brand marketing executive your handy hammer might be "20% off" discounts to spike sales.

As an PR person your handy hammer might be "email a Media Release" every time.

So, here's what I'd love you to do next ...
Grab a tea and coffee and reflect on whether you have a reflexive reaction to situations and challenges?

What's your Handy Hammer?

Sometimes it's painful to surface it and realise how narrow and habitual your solution-finding has become. But, as professionals, we all develop behavioural ruts, especially if those solutions have worked for us in the past.

The problem is when the business conditions change, when technology changes, when our competitors change, that may not be the most impactful and effective solution any more.

So, put down that hammer, and step away from the desk.

If you're lucky like me, your results will be immediate.

Exponential Thinking achieves Exponential Growth.

I know, I know. You've got tough targets and stretch goals to meet, right?

(If not, why not)

It's time to wheel out Exponential Thinking to turbo-boost Exponential Growth.

Need to achieve your target in 6 months? Nah! Achieve that in 3 months instead. How could you do that? What about 1 month?

Need to work within a budget of $x? Nah! Do it with 0.5 $x instead. How could you do that? What about 0.1 $x

You'll be surprised how simply tweaking your mindset to Exponential Thinking mode will make radical new possibilities appear.

Because constraints cause creativity.

Zooming In and Out.

My great passion is motorcycle touring. I love to see the world on two-wheels, and have done hundreds of thousands of kilometres of riding through Australia, Switzerland, Thailand, Malaysia, Singapore, Hong Kong, Burma, Nepal, and Laos.

Let's talk a bit about my last big trip, nearly 5000km criss-crossing Laos.

The road conditions are very, very patchy. And often shockingly bad. So I need to be totally focussed for every second on what's right in front of me. Scanning for the best bit of road to use. *Zoomed in.*

But, if I spend the whole time zoomed in, I might not notice that the road leads to a dead-end, a cliff without a safety barrier, or that I've taken a wrong turn and now

I'm on completely the wrong road which leads in the opposite direction to which I intended (I once ended up on the China border at Boten this way!) So, I also need to have my head up, scanning the horizon and the bigger picture. *Zoomed out.*

And you need to be the same at work. We are very good these days at zooming in to the 3rd decimal point of the sales data in the spreadsheet. Technology and software is really helping us here.

But it could be hurting us too -- because we're losing our zoom-out muscles. The ability to step back and see the wider context of the business landscape.

Zooming in we might feel we're doing things right, but zooming out we might find we're not doing the right things.

So spend some time today to take your nose out of the Excel spreadsheet and zoom out to see all the moving parts of your eco-system and value chain.

What's the bigger picture of possibilities and pitfalls you're not seeing? How does what you see zooming in relate to what you see when you zoom out? What's the connection? How you you make that connection to the future?

Snap Out of That Coma – and Think 27 Years Ahead.

Can you imagine being in a coma -- wait, that's not the bad part yet -- for 27 years? *Twenty seven!*

And Munira Abdullah's family never gave up on the fact that their tube-fed mum would one day wake up from that dreadful car accident. Then finally she did.

I read the story with my slack jaw dropping almost to the keyboard of my laptop.

As it happens my son, Justin, was born that same year 1991. So this story caused me to think about how the world has changed in that period. And how Munira has woken up into a completely changed world. (It's known as the "Rip van Winkle Effect" after the story of Rip who fell asleep for 20 years and missed the American Revolution.)

Saw a funny interview once with this greying dude who'd just been released from a very lengthy prison sentence in the US and was on a bus. The one thing he noticed was *everybody* on the phone. "What the hell is everybody talking about?" he asked, staggered by this new phenomenon.

So, apart from the iPhone, here's just some of the things we take for granted today that were not in the world in 1991:

ABS brakes for most/all car models.
Digital sensors for cameras.
Mosaic web browser (made internet surfing easy and enjoyable)
Plasma TVs
Toyota Prius hybrid car
Portable MP3 players
Stem cell transplants
Wi-fi routers
Netflix
Uber
Amazon
Google Maps
Affordable DNA genome sequencing.

And one new thing Munira will notice for sure in her native Dubai: the 828-metre tall Burj Khalifa, plus about half of the Dubai skyline.

Then of course the rapid dominance of Middle Eastern carriers such as Emirates, Etihad and Qatar which have revolutionised the dynamic of air travel.

So if you're feeling a little tired because of the breath-taking pace of change, now you know why. And things are only going to speed up from here.

Here's the question to ponder:
What will your industry look like in 27 years time?

Get your team around and do some stretch thinking about the major tectonic shifts that you think might be coming. It should surface some fascinating possibilities, and challenge some deeply entrenched assumptions. No one knows for sure, but at least it'll start you moving exponentially towards that brave new world.

Because the secret is to arrive at the future just before your customer or consumer does. Otherwise you don't have a future.

Which Lens Do You View the World Through?

My niece Sophie is in her final year of an engineering degree, and acing it (something which would never have been said about my university years).

Over dinner at my brother's place recently, we were talking about how she was enjoying engineering and what she was learning. She had learned a lot and it had changed the way she sees the world, she added.

Sophie looked out at the back yard, to where a rope swing with rubber tyre hung from a huge tree. "For example, when I look at that swing," she said, "I see the swing with force arrows pointing out from it. And when it's swinging, my god, it's just full of arrows shooting out everywhere."

I promptly moved the wine glass away from her. "I think you've had enough wine, young lady," I joked.

But it's true - we all have different perspectives, different lenses,

different reality.

I studied a lot of film-making at uni, and when I was making TV commercials as a creative director, I could never just go and watch a movie at the cinema to unwind. I was looking for story-lines, I was wondering why the director framed the shot that way, I questioned the editors cutting away from a scene too late.

That was the lens, literally, through which I saw the world.

So which lens (or lenses) do you see the world through? Be aware YOUR reality is not everyone's reality.

Same world, different viewpoint, different experiences.

This can be a strength when it's relevant, but be aware of when it might cloud your judgment. Be ready to flip viewpoint, switch to a different lens.

It might help you see the other person's point of view better, or overcome an obstacle in a challenge you're facing. Sometimes it's best to look down the opposite end of the telescope.

What's your Perception Shifting tool?

Browsing in a Sydney bookshop I came across a beautiful publication by iconic Aussie landscape photographer, Ken Duncan. Page after page of mouthwatering images that capture such spirit and sense of place.

"Always look at things from different angles," Ken advises us. "Be adventurous. Don't just fall into the obvious. Always be willing to push yourself to your limits."

He'll often stand on a suitcase, or stand on the roof of his Toyota, or even hang on a harness out of a helicopter to get greater depth and perspective. Whatever it takes to get the most dramatic and effective outcome.

Good advice for all of us as we go about our business daily.

Question for you:

How do you change perspective on your challenges and opportunities to make sure you're seeing it differently and can get a different more dramatic solution? What's YOUR suitcase or helicopter at work?

(Hint: reframing the question and defining your problem differently is about the best tool I know.)

PROVOCATION CHEAT SHEET.

(Use for Solo or Team Work.)

On the Maverick Mindset.

What's on YOUR list of Top 5 books about creativity, innovation and intrapreneurship?

Who are the BIG 5 creative role models in your life? How can you emulate their approach to help you break the glass cage of your current thinking, or see your industry from a different direction that could change the game?

Take 3 minutes now and think about what ruts you might be stuck in? What behavioural patterns are you repeating for no particular reason other than it has become your habit?

How are you going to up-skill your (and/or your team's) creative thinking skills in 2020 and beyond?

What are you really committed to? What would YOUR tattoo/s say if you got one done?

On Purpose and Culture.

Policies vs Principles: Which management style do you use and how may that be hurting your company's development of a creative culture?

View the video of JFK in action delivering his 'Man to the Moon' speech, or read the full speech text. And see how you can align your team behind you on the important mission that you and they are currently on by creating and articulating a compelling vision that they are dying to be part of. Tip: start with "I believe ..." and go from there.

What stories do you have to define who you are, who you've become, what you stand for, how you live, and how you make decisions? (Tackle it from an individual and also from a company stance.)

What might be a better job title that gets to the heart of what you *really* do and says something about your company's personality? It might help reframe how you see your important role, and what others can rightfully expect from you in that role.

How much is in this year's budget for 'experimentation'?

Where are you going to be doing your best work today? (Answer 'at my desk' is not permissible.)

You have around 240 available weekday lunch times each year. How do you plan to use them better in terms of networking for *ideas*?

What are some of the best meeting room names you've seen, or can think of??? Why not change the names of the meeting rooms in your office?

On Strategic Thinking.

Take a few minutes to think of what Legacy Thinking exists in your industry? In your company? In your business unit? What are you going to do to challenge that?

Make a list of products which are unprofitable, solutions which don't suit your core competencies, people who are not forward-compatible with your progressive values, etc. Now look at that list and ask yourself: "What *WON'T* I do today?"

Cathedral Thinking is the sort of approach with which we can transcend ordinary everyday thinking and behaviours, which can help you and your company find a more meaningful true north purpose. Take 9 minutes and enjoy this wonderful TEDx talk by Rick on "cathedral thinking." Is there something more sustainable and meaningful you should be working towards?

What are the red flags in your business or industry that you're not seeing (or choosing not to see) today? And what are you going to do about it?

What are you doing so differently and effectively that it should be a red flag to your competitors and industry model? If nothing, get onto it *now*.

What does your business plan for the Year of the Rat look like? Is it 100 pages long? Is it full of empty but important sounding buzzwords? What are you *really* trying to achieve this year? What's going to make the most impact? Focus on that. Turn that into a 9-word business plan now.

We need a new word to describe what platform-changing 'disruptive innovation' really is. What are your suggestions?

On Customer-centricity.

What business are you really, Really, REALLY in? Work this out by figuring out the ultimate emotional benefit of the benefit of your product or service's features.

How can you curate a better experience for your customers today? (Tip: start with empathy.)

How could you over-deliver on a customer or client's expectations today? Go and do that thing.

How do you and your company make sense of your world? What's your 'nose and tongue' into the customer's or consumer's market? How do you pick up trends, early warning signals?

Where's the story disconnect in your business or brand? What brand signal are you sending out that is actually sending the opposite message to customers and staff? Identify it, and fix it quickly.

On Peak Performance.

What would you never do again in order to improve your performance at work? Share and explain.

What if we put 90% of our effort into the last 10% of the job, the proposal, the product development, the manufacturing? How does that change what we do and how we do it?

How might you apply your knowledge of Intermittent Thinking to your day's work for better performance and output? (Pomodoro technique, minimum 5 minute break each hour, 2 hours of flow zone each day, etc.)

Ask yourself "What will I decide to be *curious* about on Monday morning?" and follow up on that curiosity.

Fun team question: how would you rank Coffee, Sex and Chocolate from favourite to least favourite?

Try a standing or walking meeting today. How did it go?

Who are the 'mailmen' and 'meat machines' on your team? What are you going to do to up-skill and repurpose them against AI?

How 'Open' are you? Take this free 10 minute test here (or Google 'openness test)

On Creative Confidence & Fear of Failure.

What are you most afraid of today? What's holding you back from your best performance at work and in life? Go and find your edges. What does extreme marketing look like? What does extreme process speed look like? What does extreme hiring look like?

Practice these 3 simple phrases to help you gain more creative confidence when suggesting or presenting ideas: "This is only an idea ..." or "This may sound crazy, but ..." or "This might be the idea that leads to the idea ..." They act like a defence mechanism for you.

On Creative Thinking & Problem Solving.

What's your Handy Hammer? Reflect on whether you have a reflexive reaction to certain situations and challenges and/or a favourite go-to solution?

Time to stretch your Exponential Thinking muscles. What's the time frame of the main project you're working on now? Ok, halve it. (ie, if you had 6 months, how could we do it in only 3 months? What if you only had 6 weeks, what would that look like?) What's the budget? What if that was halved, how might that look? And what if the budget was only 10%? Go on, push yourself to consider the possibilities.

Step back and zoom out: What's the bigger picture of your industry or eco-system you're not seeing? How does what you see when zooming in relate to what you see when you zoom out? What's the connection? How can you make a connection to the future?

What will your industry look like in 27 years time? Get your team around and do some stretch thinking about the major tectonic shifts that you think might be coming. It should surface some fascinating possibilities, and challenge some deeply entrenched assumptions. Allow yourself to dream and drift. Now apply the more realistic ideas to today and find the future first.

Which lens (or lenses) do you see the world through? How is this an advantage, and how and where is this a possible drawback?

How do you change perspective on your challenges and opportunities to make sure you're seeing it differently and can get a different more dramatic solution? Share some perspective shifting techniques.

-- That's all, folks! --

AFTERWORD

If you found this book interesting, stimulating or provocative, why not get Stu Lloyd in to give you The Stu Lloyd Experience at your workplace or next conference for 10 or 10,000 people?

Email: stu@hotheads-innovation.com

Sign up to The Maverick Manifesto blog here to make sure you get regular shots of Stu-ness straight to your inbox: https://www.hotheads-innovation.com/blog

Hey, did you know Stu also wears the Chief Storyteller hat at **CAT-MATDOG**? Check out how we unleash your storytelling power so you can captivate, convince and convert better. **Catmatdog.com**

ABOUT THE AUTHOR

Stu Lloyd

Born in Zimbabwe, Australian citizen Stu is celebrating 30 years at the intersection of creativity and commerce, and 20 years of transformative training in 2020.

As an advertising guy, he was a creative director for agencies such as Ogilvy& Mather, Saatchi & Saatchi, Bates, etc, before co-founding integrated agency, LloydMartin, in Singapore, which he successfully built up and sold to US-listed group DraftFCB, becoming Country Managing Director and achieving a 44% YOY top line growth against the backdrop of the Asia Financial Crisis.

Stu was a founding lecturer at the Singapore Institute of Advertising, guest lecturer at University of Washington's international business program, has addressed a UN WTO forum on innovation and trends, and MC'd a TEDx event on Creativity & Collaboration.

As Chief Hothead @ Hotheads Innovation, Stu helps Fortune 500 companies like Citibank, Adidas, Pfizer, Intel, DaimlerBenz, etc to turbocharge their creative thinking and innovation discovery skills.

As Chief Storyteller @ CATMATDOG, Stu helps Fortune 500 companies like Adobe, Accor, Citibank, Colgate-Palmolive, etc to unleash the power of their strategic storytelling and content

creation.

WIth a passion for psychology (a degree from Macquarie University and further certification in neuro-science and neuo-marketing from Copenhagen Business School) Stu often describes often himself as 'the dumbest guy in the room' in deference to the brilliant minds and people he gets to work with.

PRAISE FOR AUTHOR

"The Pefect Storyteller!"

- THE TELEGRAPH, UK.

"Stu is a rare "intellectual-doer" who boils ideas and insights down into digestible, actionable points that we can apply immediately to make us more effective, efficient and impactful in our work.

"Stu is a guide who facilitates understanding, motivates, and ultimately helps us be better at our work."

- WILL NEALY, SENIOR MANAGER, ADIDAS AMERICA.

"Absolutely compelling!"

- JOHN KERR, RADIO 2UE, AUSTRALIA.

"Whenever I spend time with Stu, I learn something new. I enjoy reading everything he publishes, and it's always very, very insightful."

- DR MARIO HARDY, CEO, PATA , AND VC/ FOUNDER.

BOOKS BY THIS AUTHOR

Killer Questions

HOW TO SHAPE BETTER QUESTIONS TO CREATE EXPLOSIVE BREAKTHROUGHS.

Learn how to Rock the New Economy with Explosive Questioning, because asking better questions is the answer for challenging the status quo in today's uncertain business world.

Full 9-step Innovation Question Formulation Canvas included.

"This book is more stimulating than a double shot of cold brew infused coffee. It is full of energy, fresh bright ideas, and reminds you how something you think is already well explored has room to grow even more. Now I can hand new engineers a strong cup of 'pure Stu' to kick-start their thinking. Make mine a double!" David Fincher, Fellow, AMD.

"Really enjoyed Killer Questions. It was like taking a peek into the minds of some of the greatest innovators in history right as they were asking these killer questions that prompted them to create history!" Kapil Kane, Head of R&D, Intel China.

"Killer Questions is a Killer Book! This has really helped with both my classroom sessions and consulting projects. Good questions stimulate good answers. Well done!" James Reinnoldt, Adj. Professor, The University of Washington.